WNBA

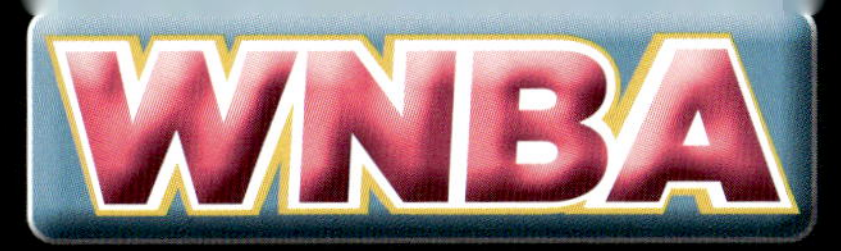

PHOENIX MERCURY

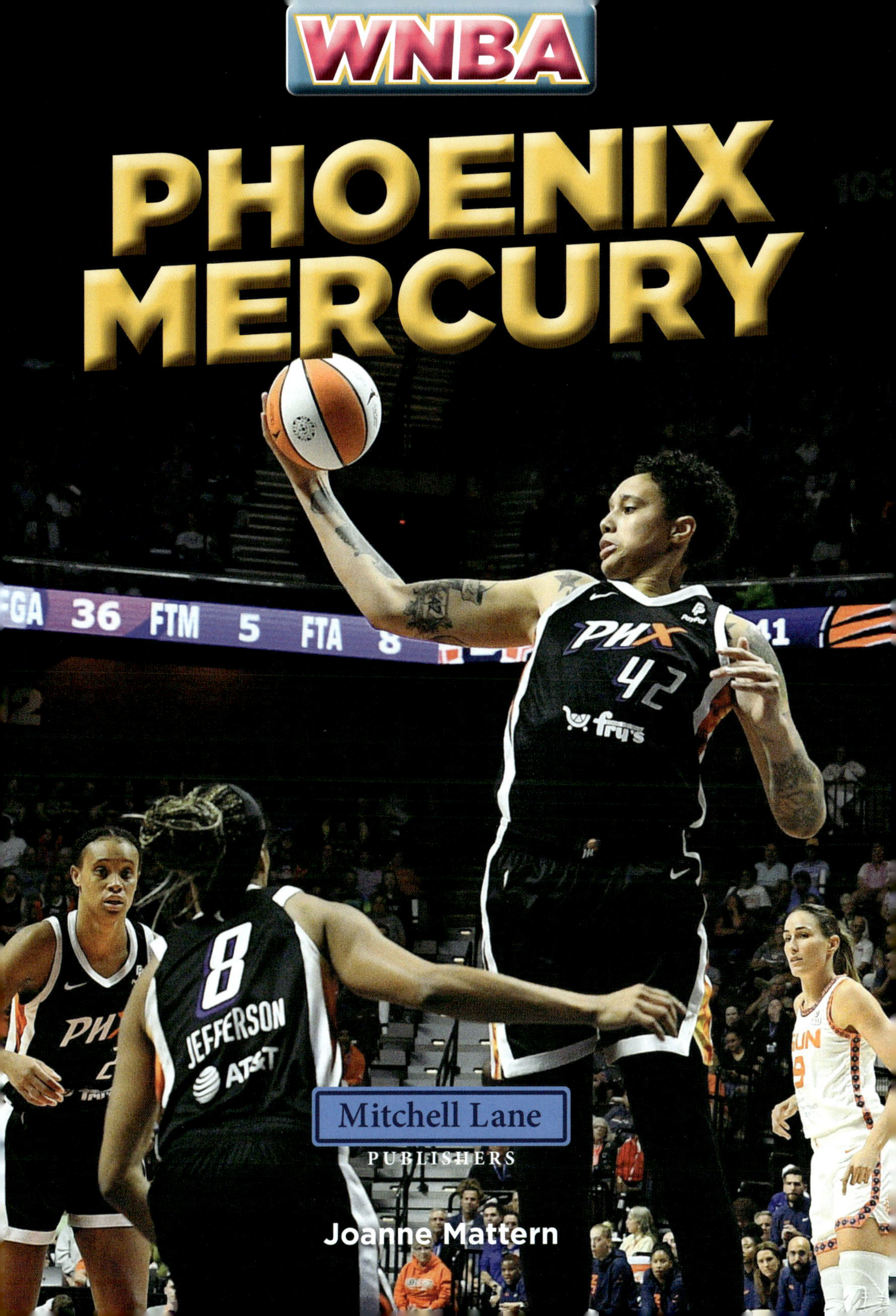

Mitchell Lane
PUBLISHERS

Joanne Mattern

Mitchell Lane
PUBLISHERS

mitchelllanepub.com

2001 SW 31st Avenue
Hallandale, FL 33009

First Edition, 2026.
Author: Joanne Mattern
Designer: Ed Morgan
Editor: Tammy Gagne

Series: WNBA
Title: Phoenix Mercury

Library bound ISBN: 979-8-89260-477-2
eBook ISBN: 979-8-89260-488-8

Photo credits: p. 21 newscom.com; balance Alamy

CONTENTS

Chapter ONE

TURNING THINGS AROUND

Diana Taurasi grabs a rebound in a game against the Chicago Sky.

The 2023 season had gotten off to a rough start for the Phoenix Mercury. Losing their first two games, the players could not seem to show their winning ways on the court. Even **point guard** Diana Taurasi, one of the Mercury's top players at the time, had made only 3 of her 18 shots. She also had 12 **turnovers** during those first two games.

But May 25 was different. On this night, Taurasi was on fire, scoring 23 points. And she wasn't the only player giving her all. Four of Taurasi's teammates scored double digits. Brittney Griner, another longtime Mercury player, racked up 19 points. Sug Sutton added 14 points, and Sophie Cunningham and Moriah Jefferson each scored 13 points for the Mercury. Phoenix soundly defeated the Minnesota Lynx 91–80.

After the game, Taurasi spoke to reporters about the change in her play. "It's not always easy, but you just stick with it, keep coming back," she told CNN. "Our whole focus here is how do we make this team better, but after our first two losses, I feel like I wasn't making the team better in a lot of ways . . . I made a **concerted** effort tonight."

Turning Things Around

Phoenix Mercury center Brittney Griner's intense focus has helped her become a star player for the team.

CHAPTER ONE

Taurasi announced her retirement in 2024. But her determination and strong sense of teamwork served as great examples of how the Mercury have succeeded in the Women's National Basketball Association (WNBA). As Taurasi noted, it hasn't always been easy. The team has had exciting triumphs but also faced some rough patches and **controversy** over the years.

Turning Things Around

FAST FACT

In the first round of the 2020 WNBA Playoffs, Shey Peddy knocked down a game winner at the buzzer to defeat the Washington Mystics 85–84. This sent the Washington Mystics home.

Chapter TWO

MAKING THEIR FOOTPRINT

The Mercury's Kelly Schumacher (right) shouts in disbelief after a foul is called on her during a game against the Sacramento Monarchs.

Based in Phoenix, Arizona, the Mercury is part of the WNBA. This basketball league was created in 1997 as the women's version of the National Basketball Association (NBA). The Phoenix Mercury was one of the league's original eight teams. Since that time, several teams have come and gone, but this one has remained.

CHAPTER TWO

The team got off to a promising start, playing its first game on June 27, 1997. It resulted in a big win over the Charlotte Sting. The Mercury made the playoffs in its first two seasons, but it wasn't until 2007 that the team won the WNBA Championship. That year, Phoenix beat the Detroit Shock in five games.

In 2009, Mercury team members became WNBA champions again. This time, they defeated the Indiana Fever to win the title. After a few losing seasons, the Mercury rose back to the top in 2014 with an astonishing 29–5 record. They ended that season by winning the WNBA Championship with a victory over the Chicago Sky.

The Mercury play at the Footprint Center in downtown Phoenix. This **venue** holds more than 17,000 people. It is also the home of the NBA's Phoenix Suns.

Making Their Footprint

FAST FACT

Footprint Center is often called the Purple Palace because both the Mercury's and Suns' uniforms are this color.

CHAPTER TWO

Both the Mercury and the Suns feel strongly about giving back to the Phoenix community. The teams partnered to create the Phoenix Suns/Phoenix Mercury Foundation. This organization helps Arizona **nonprofit** groups with their funding.

In 2023, executive director Sarah Krahenbuhl told the press, "The Phoenix Suns/Phoenix Mercury Foundation celebrates the positive **impact** both the Suns and Mercury teams make on and off the court." She shared that the money the foundation provides makes a difference "in the lives of children across Arizona." The foundation also hosts community events, player appearances, and charity drives. It has raised more than $43 million in funds.

Making Their Footprint

The Mercury's Kahleah Copper fights to make a two-point shot against players from the Minnesota Lynx.

Chapter THREE

THE BEST PERSON FOR THE JOB

Cheryl Miller was one of the stars of the U.S. women's basketball team at the 1984 Olympics.

The Phoenix Mercury's first head coach was Cheryl Miller. A former player for the University of Southern California, Miller is a member of the Basketball Hall of Fame. Miller coached Phoenix for its first four seasons. She led the Mercury to a 70–52 record over those seasons, and she also guided the team to three playoff appearances.

CHAPTER THREE

As of 2024, seven of the Mercury's twelve head coaches have been women. In 2023, the Mercury named Nate Tibbetts as its head coach. He also became the highest-paid coach in the WNBA when he took the job. His **salary** is $1 million a year.

Many people thought this amount was too high since Tibbetts had no WNBA coaching experience. In his official team bio, Tibbetts shared that his father had coached women's basketball. The new WNBA coach also listed "girl dad" as one of his accomplishments. Some people worried that he wasn't qualified for the job.

The Best Person for the Job

Mercury player Natasha Cloud takes a shot in a game against the Minnesota Lynx.

FAST FACT

There is a wide pay gap between the WNBA and the NBA. The top WNBA player salaries are in the hundreds of thousands of dollars. The top NBA player salaries are in the tens of millions of dollars.

"I'm sensitive to the situation," Tibbetts said at a press conference announcing his arrival. "I know I'm one of only three male head coaches in the WNBA. . . . I know that people are questioning it, and agree or disagree, I'm going to do the best job that I can and do the best for our players and try to put them in positions to get better and be successful."

The Phoenix Mercury players stood behind Tibbetts. In 2024, Brittney Griner told the *Arizona Republic* that Tibbetts was "challenging me to play a little bit different. . . . That's something I always want to add to my game." Only time will tell if Tibbetts is the best person to lead the Phoenix Mercury.

The Best Person for the Job

Phoenix head coach Nate Tibbetts directs the action from the sidelines during a game.

Chapter FOUR

THE MERCURY'S STAR PLAYERS

Diana Taurasi had been an important part of the Mercury since its early days.

The Phoenix Mercury has had many outstanding players over the years. One of the best was Diana Taurasi. After several losing seasons, the Mercury chose Taurasi in the first round of the 2004 WNBA Draft. She helped turn the team around. Taurasi scored more career points than any other WNBA player with an astonishing 10,518 at the end of 2024. Even after twenty years with the team, Taurasi still routinely scored double digits per game.

CHAPTER FOUR

Center Brittney Griner joined the Mercury in 2013. Like Taurasi, she has remained a powerful part of the team since becoming a member. In her **debut** with the team, Griner became the first player in WNBA history to dunk the ball twice in one game. In 2014, she set the WNBA record for blocked shots in a game with 11.

Griner lost an entire season with the Mercury when she was imprisoned in Russia for a minor **offense** in February 2022. Like many WNBA players, she had traveled to Russia to play in a basketball league there during the WNBA off-season. The United States worked hard to get her back home that December.

The Mercury's Star Players

Diana Taurasi (left) and Kahleah Copper (right)

FAST FACT

Mercury players Kahleah Copper, Brittney Griner, and Diana Taurasi were members of the 2024 U.S. Olympic basketball team.

CHAPTER FOUR

Griner returned to the Mercury in 2024. She is the team's top rebounder and its second-leading scorer, behind Taurasi. The Mercury's general manager, Nick U'Ren, said, "[Griner] has been a **stalwart** of the Phoenix Mercury and Phoenix community for the past decade, and we are excited that she will be with us as we build a team that can compete every night on both ends of the floor. We know winning is what's most important to her and that she can help lead us this year."

Although the team has struggled in recent years, the Phoenix Mercury keeps fighting for those wins. The dedication of the Mercury's players and coaches has inspired fans to continue supporting the team and to expect great things in the future.

The Mercury's Star Players

Brittney Griner refuses to let opponent Teaira McCowan stop her from scoring during a game against the Dallas Wings.

GLOSSARY

center
A basketball player who plays near the basket, often the tallest member of the team

concerted
Performed with the assistance or cooperation of another person

controversy
An issue drawing strong and differing viewpoints

debut
The first performance of a player

impact
A strong effect on someone or something

nonprofit
Set up for a purpose other than making money

offense
A violation of the law

point guard
A basketball player who brings the ball up the court and sets up offensive plays

salary
A set amount of pay for regular work

stalwart
Someone who is dependably strong

turnovers
Instances during a basketball game when one team loses possession of the ball to the other team

venue
A building or space where a game takes place

SLAM DUNK WNBA TRIVIA

- The first coach to lead the Phoenix Mercury to a championship was Paul Westhead in 2007. In 1980, he coached the Los Angeles Lakers all the way to the NBA Championship. Phoenix's win made Westhead the first person to win a championship title in both the WNBA and the NBA.
- The Phoenix Mercury's mascot is Scorch. According to his story, he was born on the planet Mercury and was drawn to Phoenix when he heard the team's "Mighty Mercury" fan chant.
- In 2023, the Mercury added a second inflatable mascot named Fuego. The word *Fuego* means "fire" in Spanish.
- Phoenix Mercury fans are known as the X-Factor.
- The team has retired former player Penny Taylor's number 13 jersey. She was a key player in two of the Mercury's championship wins.
- As of 2024, the Phoenix Mercury has qualified for the WNBA Playoffs fifteen times.

FIND OUT MORE

IN PRINT

Brown, Monica, *Diana Taurasi*. Philomel Books, 2022.

Davidson, B. Keith. *WNBA*. Crabtree Publishing, 2022.

Helt, Julianna. *Minnesota Lynx*. Mitchell Lane Publishers, 2026.

ON THE INTERNET

***Phoenix Mercury*, n.d.**
https://mercury.wnba.com.

"Phoenix Mercury," *ESPN*, n.d.
www.espn.com/wnba/team/_/name/phx/phoenix-mercury.

"Phoenix Mercury," *FOX Sports*, n.d.
www.foxsports.com/wnba/phoenix-mercury-team.

INDEX

About the Author

Joanne Mattern has loved basketball since she was a little girl shooting hoops in her driveway and playing at the local YMCA. She has written numerous nonfiction books for children, and sports biographies are among her favorites to research and write. Joanne lives in New York State with her family.